■ SCHOLASTIC

News

Nonfiction Readers®

See Inside the White House

By Marge Kennedy

Children's Press®
An Imprint of Scholastic Inc.
New York Toronto London Auckland Sydney
Mexico City New Delhi Hong Kong
Danbury, Connecticut

These content vocabulary word builders are for grades 1–2.

Subject Consultant: Eli J. Lesser, MA, Director of Education,
National Constitution Center, Philadelphia, Pennsylvania

Reading Consultant: Cecilia Minden-Cupp, PhD, Early Literacy Consultant and Author,
Chapel Hill, North Carolina

Photographs © 2009: Alamy Images/Art Kowalsky: 7; AP Images: 23 bottom left (Pablo Martinez Monsivais), 9 top (Evan Vucci); Corbis Images: cover, 4 bottom left, 16 (Brooks Kraft), 17 (Paul Morse/Reuters); Getty Images: 5 bottom left, 6 (Peter Gridley), 5 top left, 8 (Time Life Pictures/Stringer); John Zweifel/Kathleen Culbert-Aguilor: 20, 21; National Geographic Image Collection/Joe Scherschel: 23 top left; The Image Works/Photri/Topham: 23 bottom right; White House Historical Association: back cover, 1, 4 top, 14, 15 (Erik Kvalsvik), 2, 4 bottom right, 5 top right, 5 bottom right, 9 bottom, 10, 11, 12, 13, 18, 19, 23 top right.

Series Design: Simonsays Design!
Art Direction, Production, and Digital Imaging: Scholastic Classroom Magazines

Library of Congress Cataloging-in-Publication Data

Kennedy, Marge M., 1950-
See Inside the White House / Marge Kennedy.
    p. cm. — (Scholastic news nonfiction readers)
Includes bibliographical references and index.
ISBN 13: 978-0-531-21097-0 (lib. bdg.)   978-0-531-22434-2 (pbk.)
ISBN 10: 0-531-21097-9 (lib. bdg.)   0-531-22434-1 (pbk.)
1. White House (Washington, D.C.)—Juvenile literature. 2. House furnishings—(Washington, D.C.)—Juvenile literature. 3. Interior decoration—Washington (D.C.)—Juvenile literature. 4. Washington (D.C.)—Buildings, structures, etc.—Juvenile literature. I. Title.
F204.W5K4558 2009
975.3—dc22   2008038924

CONTENTS

WORD HUNT

Look for these words as you read. They will be in **bold**.

Blue Room
(bloo room)

Oval Office
(**oh**-vuhl **off**-iss)

Red Room
(red room)

4

china
(**chye**-nuh)

Gold Room
(gohld room)

White House
(wite houss)

Yellow Oval Room
(**yel**-oh **oh**-vuhl room)

Let's Look Inside!

Many people see the outside of the **White House**. What would you see on the inside?

You would see many rooms. Each room has a name that tells you something about it.

White House

The President lives and works in the White House. It is in Washington, D.C.

Some rooms get their names from what is in them. In the **China** Room, there are china plates.

The plates are used for eating at the White House.

china

The dishes in the China Room are inside glass cases. The cases protect the china.

Do you think there is real gold in the **Gold Room**?

Yes, there is! Dishes covered in gold are kept here.

Gold Room

Look for the gold dishes in the case on the wall.

Some rooms in the White House are named for their colors.

There is a **Red Room**. The President sometimes gives small parties here.

Red Room

How many red things can you find in this room?

Can you guess what this room is called?

It is the **Blue Room**! The President sometimes meets important visitors here.

Blue Room

Some rooms in the White House get their names from their shape.

The **Oval Office** is the most important one. That is where the President works.

Oval Office

Can you see the oval shape of the President's office?

One room in the White House is named for its color *and* its shape. It is called the **Yellow Oval Room**.

There are 132 rooms inside the White House. Now you have seen six of them!

Yellow Oval Room

You can see part of the oval
shape if you look at the ceiling.

A MINI TOUR OF THE WHITE HOUSE

This is a model, or small copy, of the White House. Take a close look! You will find some of the rooms shown in this book.

1 The Yellow Oval Room

2 The Lincoln Bedroom

3 The State Dining Room

4 The Red Room

5 The Blue Room

6 The Green Room

7 The East Room

8 The China Room

9 The Gold Room

Would you like to visit the White House in person? The White House is open for group tours. To learn more, ask an adult to go to www.whitehouse.gov/history/tours

YOUR NEW WORDS

Blue Room (bloo room) a room in the White House with blue carpets and curtains

china (**chye**-nuh) thin, fancy dishes

Gold Room (gohld room) a room in the White House where dishes made of gold-covered silver are kept

Oval Office (**oh**-vuhl **off**-iss) the President's office in the White House

Red Room (red room) a room in the White House with red walls and furniture

White House (wite houss) the building where the President lives and works

Yellow Oval Room (**yel**-oh **oh**-vuhl room) a room in the White House with an oval shape and yellow walls and curtains

FOUR MORE WHITE HOUSE ROOMS

The East Room

The Green Room

The State Dining Room

The Lincoln Bedroom

INDEX

FIND OUT MORE

Book:

Debnam, Betty. *A Kid's Guide to the White House.* Kansas City: Andrews McMeel Publishing, 1997.

Website:

White House Kids
www.whitehouse.gov/kids/tour

MEET THE AUTHOR

Marge Kennedy fondly remembers visiting the White House with her daughter.